Bird Silence

POEMS *by* **Matthew Roth**

Bird Silence

Published by Woodley Press
Washburn University,
Topeka, Kansas 66621

Library of Congress Cataloging-in-Puublication Data
Roth, Matthew.
Bird Silence / Matthew Roth. — 1st ed.

ISBN 978-0-9817334-4-9

CONTROL NUMBER 2009933387

Printed in the United States of America

FIRST EDITION

DESIGN AND LAYOUT
David Kasparek
VISUALMENTALSTIMULI.COM

Acknowledgments

Many thanks to the following journals, in
which many of these poems first appeared,
some in slightly different forms:

32 Poems
American Literary Review
Antioch Review
Blue Mesa Review
Coe Review
Fence
Minnesota Review
Passages North
Phoebe
Poetry Motel
Quarter After Eight
South Ash Press
Stonework (online)
Verse

Some of these poems also appeared in a
limited-edition chapbook, *Occasional Hats,*
(Scramble Press, 2001).

I wish to thank all of the generous, talented people who
in innumerable ways contributed to the making of this
book, including Bruce Bond, Albert Goldbarth, Jeanine
Hathaway, John Poch, Chad Davidson, Jim Huffman,
Richard Wagle, and Tom Noyes. Thanks to David
Kasparek for his inspired design work, and to Laura
Lee Washburn for her keen editorial eye. Special thanks
to my wife, Kerry, and to my two children, Ella and Silas.

Table of Contents

One

Two

Three

for **Kerry**

One

The Rumor Mill

Shut doors not quite shut. The vents.
The circulating air. The sign above
the window reads *We Never Close.*

Inside, this vast blast furnace
with the great glass doors.
The better to witness the burning.

So many stories.
So many tiny, box-like rooms,
each with a tiny desk,
a tiny fragment of the self.

The mad composer's genitalia peek
through the door at his cheating heart.

The faded starlet is at last composed.
Only her breasts still reside
many stories beneath her.

On the fourteenth floor, the lone
cleaning lady stops to rest.

The broom without bristles.
No wastebaskets here.

What, then, to do
with all the wasted paper,
the human hair and limbs?

One pocket of her dress
is full with seeds.

The other is ripe with birds.

No Mark

There was a high stone wall
separating our land—the small yard,
half sand, where my father grew

tomatoes—from the royal preserve.
Years ago, I was told, the king himself
hunted there among well-ordered trees,

made camp by the stream that coils
through its heart. There was even—
still it's there, though overgrown—

a small orchard of sweet peaches
and apricots. Now thickets
lie stripped by a tangle of deer,

the high wall my father disappeared
behind one day overthrown
by slow degrees of frost and thaw.

Many days, I have stepped through
a breach, found myself in that
odd, forbidden state, my own

and not my own. And once,
beneath the government
of a twin row of sycamores,

I found the hoofprints of a horse,
each shallow C filled in
with tarnished bronze. Amazed,

I followed, until the hooves
stopped short in a clearing
by the edge of a small reflecting pool.

A stone in its middle made it look
like a human eye. To one side
a thick-trunked magnolia leaned.

This must have been April,
the water clotted with pink,
fleshy petals. I stood wondering

when all at once the surface cleared
a moment, and I started
at the sudden flare of my face

peering into the pool, or well,
or deep oubliette, where I lay
staring up at the shadowed face,

which hovered like a stone
in the sky's open eye. Somehow
I knew, whoever it was,

he had not come to save me.

Lucky Day

There is a cat who picks stocks
with his paw of terrible forethought.
Or you're perfectly human

and can't stop thinking
like a cat. How nice the sun feels
streaming through the window mornings.

You would like nothing more
than to eat a good breakfast,
go back to sleep for awhile,

then eat a good breakfast.
Did I mention this cat is a millionaire?
You might be rich too if you were orange,

if your eyes were more human.
You can play with the electric mouse.
But alas, the new cat toys are all about loss.

In this way, they resemble the old cat toys.
Then your wife calls to you, asking
for a quarter. You reach into your pocket,

pluck it out with nimble fingers.
Then you reach into your pocket again,
just because you can.

Mortuary Fish

The mortician's boy is a genius
with a football underneath his arm.
He's got that shimmy in his hips,
can freeze a linebacker just like that,
as he slides by into the open field
stretching out before him, empty
and uncluttered as the morning table.

His dad has never missed a snap, is proud
to tell you so. Come Friday night,
he turns off all the lights, locks
the large oak doors, then walks
the five blocks toward the orange glow
that pulses above the field, above the cries
that arc through the night,
aimless as errant passes.

In the darkened basement,
his instruments begin the hard task
of forgetting. Slow fish burrow
the outlines of their tank.
The only lights are the dull,
unblinking lights
just behind their eyes.

How Memory Works

One giant slab of morning light
crashes down the narrow street
like a whale struck in a shipping lane.

The scientists come wearing rubber gloves
and hip waders. They heave it onto the sidewalk
and have at it with their dull gray instruments.

Soon, its organs are spilled across the ground
like Gettysburg's dead. They slice open
the stomach and find everything

the light consumed: the white tablecloth
bruised with wine, the two a.m. feeding,
the knife and the gun, brown nut of sleep

cracked open, bowed heads of flowers,
still fragrant, asleep in their beds.
By the time I arrive almost nothing is left.

Every article of interest has been carted away
to far-off labs for further study. So I go, without
thinking even to touch its dim remainders,

lying there on the concrete like twilight—
not thinking until now, two weeks hence,
standing here in the pre-dawn rain,

I look down and spy something
glinting off my black boots
like a tiny flower of daylight,

which it is.

Europa

He's a musician, so he understands
how quickly the imperishable
can betray itself. Lately, when he sits
in the tub, the water level doesn't change,
and his battleships have all been refitted,
chartered out by sad Sicilian fishermen
who dance slow circles
around one another
singing into their hands
so that each note returns.

Like them, he has written a song
about boats, but as with all such songs,
it is really about death,
about a woman who grew
to the size of a continent
and of the people who lived there,
how they worshipped what they could not
understand: the shifting ground,
its violent eruptions,
the ghosts of all the weary men
gone down to the sea in ships.

In an Occupied Land

No revolution here. No matter
the gunshots ringing out each night
inside your eyes, the nerve-net fouled
by a bad dream or two. Your lungs
hang out on street corners all day
smoking cheap cigars. It's okay,
they assure you, this is our job, really.

The hip-bone marries the thigh-bone,
they give birth to three sad knuckles
and the bone of contention.
In the narrowing corridors
of your last best artery, your blood
sells secrets for nickels
to buy you a grave.

What has already happened
was for your own good.
Don't trouble yourself
with what comes next—
your heart sitting cross-legged
at the foot of a tree with its empty bowl,
that bottle of port it's been saving
it seems like forever.

The Natural World

There is not, for example,
a spoon large enough
to unionize its individual molecules.
What chance would they have anyway
in the new world disorder?

Even the frost that used to hide
the moon's cold indiscretions
has left our windows bare.
This is forever: television
makes love to your firstborn son

immoderately. How, you ask,
could this happen here?
My friend, walk in the woods at dusk
and see everywhere the gallows
locked inside the whims of trees.

From the Stamp
Collection of P. Monk

#72 is the Archduke of the Grand Duchy of etc. a quite noble chin and one wispy lock of brown hair curling round his ear which is pink as if he just stepped in from a ride on his donkey which he rode through the snow to the late Tudor style house of the artist Borodov who noticed the light clinging there on the side of his head and so put it down and we know this because we stayed in his palace the four of us crammed in his bed with our feet sticking out listening to the tour guide who chain-smoked and belched the national song and didn't mind if he did have a bit of our cheese thank you very much this is not on the stamp.

Money

My pockets spring open with marsupial alacrity, its mere presence a happy coupling of bread and clean bed linen, wine and the heimliched remains of a dubious ancestry.

To have and have lots, the good factory humming its simple song of the ledger . . .

My father: "Next time Uncle Larry pulls a quarter out your nose, kick him in the balls and run."

They were money launderers, my young ears heard, and I thought how pleasant that job must be, cleaning each bill, wiping away the sweat from a hundred too-tight fists, stroking their soft, clean backs, like rabbits.

Long ago, when money was beardless, it made cruel alliances with charity, with villagers who still whispered at night so the stars wouldn't hear.

Promise Me

A cup of softest lint
to wash my face.

Two dimes to rub together
on the coldest day.

One bird in the bush.

Okay, one bush.

A heart that beats
a beat just right for dancing.

A personality stamped
Special Blend For Export.

A personality!

Just these few simple things.
A cup. A bird. A dance.

The moon, for instance.

Lysippan Proportions

At all times I carry a pin in my pocket, a charm and a reminder of the world's cruel deal with itself. I too have a tiny head, which makes me seem eight feet tall. To support myself, I'm translating a lost Viking epic, but who reads them anymore, even when these Vikings have bad drug habits and give each other high-fives after sacking Normandy. At last, someone slips a note beneath my closet door. *Come hither with your flasket of guts.* Peculiar. But the day is looming heavy with castoff bird feathers. I can't even see across the street to the dry goods emporium, to the maker of hammers: *tack, rubber, ball-peen, claw.* Then I'm outside running because it's under me, closing on me like a poisonous lily, like a corset of bees. I run past the darkened shop windows: *tackrubberballpeen-claw.* Past the careless pastry chef licking his white fingers unaware. Also, I have no shoes. Perfectly thirsty, I am a translator of Viking epics. It eats me. Me and my brand-new pants, the French ones without any pockets.

Edema

The man dying in the white room climbs out
his window, down eight stories to the hospital garden,
to the sunken garden, the vine-choked garden
is how he thinks of it, or sometimes the garden of *cleome:*
the one flower he remembers.

Today, capsized—*half-dead*, he thinks—on a bed
of white flowers he cannot recall, a red bicycle.
So he rides into the countryside, beyond the gray river,
down to the green valley where he is certain
the people kill only what eats them.

By the time his lungs fill with blood, he is back
in the white room, the white nurse standing over him.
Not long, she says, and he thinks
he too should say something of interest.
Just then he remembers: *gardenias.*

Upon Receiving the Word

One heron rises
from the mist of his swamp
like the lowest note
from an old man's cello.

Slow bubble of morning
blooms afternoon.

The volunteer fireman finds a match,
strikes it, hesitates,
then pinches out the small flame
between practiced fingers.

Later, when he returns to look
for what he left behind,
he finds only a note.

Don't ask, it says.

Love,
The Match

The Present Bird

These days we cannot even wake
in a house not on fire.
So quickly extinguished

by the failure of wishing.
I have a bird I can confess
but never show you. Its bones

I found clawing the fire pit.
Each new day a feather,
a dab of unspeakable glue.

But it's too cold to fly, love,
backward anyway. And tomorrow
is roaring again in its furnace.

Pay no attention to a notion
of birds. Even my dead one,
today, can't say where it's going.

Tooly's Regards

When the postcard arrives I take a minute
to closely examine the white horse,
the black wooden carriage, the hayrack
upstage left, heavy with its labor.

So that's how you live now, Tooly,
who left so many years ago without warning.
And how do I know it is you, since the postcard
bears only this photograph and my address,
written in a careful hand?

Because, Tooly, the carriage is a funeral carriage.
Because rain gathers in the clouds, which boil
on the horizon, and the hay will be ruined,
that is easy to see. It will rot
and its mice will gather up their young,
return to the wide, sweet-scented fields
from which they first were lifted,
helpless as the grass they left behind.

The Poet, Mid-Career

Against life's alluvial sediment,
or a middle way poured of blunt excess,
against a renewal of beautiful sympathy
for unkempt girls, or a failure

of bright trumpets, I set myself.
These generosities I searched for once
in a market, in a fury, breathing underwater
just to prove no fear of dying.

A little inhuman dance to please
the waitresses in hell? This is the way
my poetry deplaned, with a tiny feather plume
on its cowboy hat, mostly sober

between ten and two. Those days
even the dusky hatefulness of bank tellers
could not make one poem
examine its shoes. The shade beneath

my butterfly net was enough for them.
They didn't eat much. Little poems,
I remember you as if you were
yesterday, and fondly too, though I know

of the suicides you practiced in the dark
when you thought no one saw you.
An unhealthy desire for a dramatic end,
the doctors said. It's okay, I used to feel

the same. These days, my poems
have learned to relax, have a little more
wine, lean slowly into the white space
of a page, blackened without end.

Directions

It's a ruined sky that makes us
bearable, like pinching yourself to forget
the ache inside your head,

to forget how good we are
at hurting each other
on any given day—this day

included, rolling across Kansas,
four hundred miles with the angry mouth
of a storm opening up in the west.

I drive while you scowl and I swear
I'd try to be a bigger man if the wipers
worked better, if the lightning didn't

cause our turgid promenade of daily trials
to seem suddenly insignificant. Do you know
what lightning can do to a person?

My love, it has nothing to do
with happiness or the dry cleaning
or the way we can't think of anything

to say afterwards, when we're both lying
there, dry-mouthed in the sweat
of a lengthening silence. It seems like hours

since we passed an exit. That's why I want you
to look at the map, for god's sake!
I'm sorry. I shouldn't have said it

that way. But we're lost, or the storm
has done something to the way we see,
or there is no storm, just a red sun flaring

the sky's pollution, and no map, no chance
of losing our way, no direction but the one
we chose way back at the very beginning.

Sonnet

The truancy of this color, a feather held to light, and
the darkening of sound as it goes, lower, folding like
a star, a long bell in the after-dinner ear, *my love, my
rose,* I sometimes said. You threw up a little. To be
accurate is all (this errancy, this color) you ever asked
of me and still I can't re-scribe for you the swivel of
an hour or the little sound an orange makes when I
break it in my hands. Remove my hands. Remove the
ornate memory of hands. Give back the feather, the very
bird, light takes from grief to grief—I'm sorry—leaf to
leaf. Nothing may touch you: *love, rose.* Nothing is safe.

The Descent

State media reported that more than 10,000 small migratory birds died mysteriously last week, dropping "like rain" from the sky.

We thought it was hailing that night. In the morning, we walked outside and saw them. Nobody made a noise about our tendencies toward wishing. My neighbor hid his mouth with a hand. Seeing that is not what makes us a community. All night the quilts grew heavier and heavier. We thought it was hailing. Somebody found them in a book. Bohemian Waxwing, *Bombycílla gárrulus*. The black eye-mask, the terminal band. We thought the heavens were opening up. Five hundred when we finally stopped numbering their dead.

In the morning, we walked outside and saw them. My neighbor crushed a lame one beneath his heel. All night I had dreamed I was flying in a cloud. Only the beating of wings told me where I was. I began striking him, and he fell to the ground. That is not what makes us a community. The cloud's blanket kept pushing us lower. We saw the houses and remembered what it was like before we turned from that. Somebody found a book. We were not in the narrative. When the last bag was full, I said we would have to buy more. When we reached them, they said they had never seen anything like us.

The Possible

I.

Day blooms. The dew-soaked
haystack steams against

its dissolution. If you thrust
your hand inside, your right hand

inside, you will feel it beginning.
If you lie there your body

will make its own fire.

II.

The brook inherits a sunstruck meadow.
Its rushes bow their heads to know

the cool passing of blood, root-song,
their swimming underground.

If we drink this water, our mouths will,
colder, quiver before breaking

a word.

In the Canyon of Forgotten Makers

i.

we pilot the little house
call it the death of weather

from here is an invitation,
a way of seeing outside
our lives incessantly

from here we observe
the vast array of obscenities
painted and/or incised
on the general landscape

most were manufactured so
will not desire or obtain
the fragile bone structure
we look for in, say,
a champion racehorse

but the obscene never fails to reform
because language is selective
forgetting, knowing one thing again
and again until only that seems true

a body   a body

of these people and events
one might suspect
they only love what keeps them

ii.

any arrangement is philosophical
not simply a beautiful collection

is not discreet symmetry
the foundation
for responsible government

green lawn and cul-de-sac
each bright selection balances

sparrow   flower   plum

we signed for them this morning
we can sign for most anything

iii.

we love our little house
how hard it works for us

criss-crossing the frozen lake
of daylight, only answering
to our singular whistle

we make a show
of gasping each morning
the bay window kicks open
a nest of bright children
impossibly lit

so we steer another way
keep looking out for something
that does not anticipate us

iv.

everything anticipates us

these chairs were made
to bear a weight our bodies
only now come into

as the house pushes tomorrow
a parcel of hours
wrapped in the near-
drowned light of the possible

stopping   not stopping

obscene manuscript
of this voyage and telling

v.

like an aborted Christmas
we squeal appearances

our house among houses
moves slowly along
the city planning

each street lamp spits
a little light   a little rain

the ornamental shade trees
calling out for a name

someone will inscribe them
someone always does

vi.

when at last we cross the river
swirling black in the eyes
of the pale-faced ferryman
arrive at the place that calls itself

HERE

and the little house grinds
to a halt in the concrete
light of evening

we swallow the word
we did not know
we wished

outside, wading waist-deep
into the shadows
of the abandoned city
its air becomes us

in our mouths, the word begins
to tick, a clock keeping time
in small measure

vii.

in small measure
an hour is not
out of breath

in its own light
the word breeds
the city greens
to our touch

on the high roof garden
a moonflower sorts the dark
pearl pool, wet mouth unfolding
becoming a language we thought
died long ago without wishing

and a name runs quick fingers
through the night-damp hair
of its own dear presence

viii.

we call out our names
the lost city calls back

we call and call
until it seems we
first were called

the city gave to us
our voices, scooped out
for the revelation of weight

as wooden bowls
might dream of rain

in the city
each barren surface speaks
its own unbroken dialect

from this one voice
the echoes multiply
surface to surface
(dust to dust)

a chorus chanting

not to us   who are we
each to each   (our name)

ix.

it is hard now
to recall the little house
whose walls once kept us
bright and numbered

it is hard now
to remember our bodies
whose limbs were made only
for care and feeding

so we wander in the echo
of our one voice
our thousand tongues

in the city of good neighbors
without government or angels

in the canyon of forgotten makers
the starfall of our one name
our lamp and our witness

may its light refuse our surface
our cold division of air

may our carol be not flesh
but the silence of flesh

may we find our one birth
in the hollow bell of this calling

Two

Hearse

I.

a word
and I begin
to see
     (a field and its farmer
     (spring planting
     (a bag of seed
     (black soil turning beneath the rake
     (dew on the horse becoming steam

a fellow he could be
anyone even my own
father is unremarkable
inside the daily weather

he this man and to
his horse he secures
(glinting) the teeth of this
his *herse* his harrow
     "the same word which,
     in a different group of senses,
     has now the form HEARSE."

in a different group
the scene re-corrects
in the ear and eye
this hardy variety

we grow and tend
and here the farmer stops

himself to listen as if
he heard his name

far off the way
my father (eighteen) says
he stopped his own
hard harrowing saw

the bombers plowing
overhead black lines
all one direction he said
he knew the meaning

So here is the part
wherein the farmer sees
the columns coming
(glinting) across the mead

therefore, exhibit:

II.

The Breach

it could have meant anything
and no reason we can see
or sense how the word survives
by grim necessity perhaps
so farmer hustles to
and beneath some banner
with other men makes
ready for the enemy

just here where the mean
defense dissolves a need
to fill that space against
and towards its own absence

a word begins (in place of)
to be—his herse, turned up
to pierce, became *cheval-de-frise*
laid in to lance

"to incommode the march as
    well of the horse, as the infantry."
    —Chambers, *Cycl.*

to incommode—both tooth
and word cutting themselves
on soil and seed now sinking
into the world made flesh

and bone the skeleton
of a different sense

He kembyd his heer wt an
hierche in stede of a combe.
—Caxton's Trans. of Ovid

plow beaten into sword
and so not just

a keen defense
but soon "a form
of battle array"
three times as deep

as wide the "Hearse
Battell"— *W. Barriffe, Military Discipline*
forms its lines to strike
against the root it can't recall

III.

> Hearse: "a triangular frame somewhat similar
> in form to the ancient harrow, designed to
> carry candles, and used at the service of
> *Tenebrae* on Easter Eve."

Good Friday
my father (forty-five)
black robe and stole
ignites the candle

we will pass from
each to each
a silent liturgy
of heat and light

ties us to what if not
this word this word
whose one sense went
to war whose other

like my father went
in stede to church
to the service and orders
of a different sense

a flame we pass
from each to each
> *Vas ad aquam benedictam.*
> *Hercia ad tenebras.* —Synod of Exeter, 1287

this too has a name
a way of being
> *Benedictio ignis*
blessing of fire

IV.

> *By-fore a tombe, that new was dyghte . . .*
> *There-on an herse, sothely to saye, Wyth*
> *an [hundred] tappers lyghte.*
> —*Le Morte de Arthure*

this word that went
two ways and came
to rest again inside
the same black space

that claims both
Christ and Christian
could not escape
(like Christ) that tomb

and so became its
ornament: "an elaborate framework originally
                intended to carry lighted tapers and
                other decorations over the bier or
                coffin while placed in the church
                at funerals."

container
and contained   *Bold Arches pierses thrugh the*
                   mid-hoast and strewes the way with
"pall   *herses.*—Heywood, Troy, 1609
bier
coffin
vaguely, a tomb, grave, or"

a word to bear
more words

The nexte daye his hearse was sett upe . . .
covered with blacke . . . garnyshed with
scogeons and with yelowe pynyons full
of blacke lyons.
—J. Hooker, *Life of Sir P. Carew,* 1575

V.

black lines move past
the coffin my father
sees it carried to
the hearse whose owner

PAUL BURNS JR., UNDERTAKER
opens the door and asks
my father (seventy)
to step inside

the new custom
Cadillac "fully loaded"
he says and shows how
each passenger controls

his own temperature
and angle of recline
"the standard bearer
of the industry"

is this then where
a word might go
to spend its own
eternity scribing

the cool remove
of each one's own
felicitous atmosphere
death as climate control

who knows what end
or what corruption
began the breath
that made it first

to break a surface
to make a good thing
grow and then
to break again for want

of life or country
a black lineage
I bend to trace
from seed to husk

and still cannot hold
it breaks again
as if to say this is
the one condition

we cannot amend or make
our own except to lie
inside it once to breathe
its pooling atmosphere

until that too is ours
and claims us
like a remnant acre
where I imagine still

my father not yet
in heaven stops
his harrowing sky-eyed
begins to run to

leap beneath the lines
that score this scene
a grand staff
whose music drowns him

(always) out he looks
so small against that
ceaseless furrowing
I see his face his mouth

but cannot hear
for all the world
his breathless voice
that word he keeps repeating

Easter Morning

God is teaching us that we must live as
men who can get along very well without
Him. The God who is with us is the God
who forsakes us.

—Dietrich Bonhoeffer

Two bodies were discovered early this
morning in a culvert beneath Interstate 81.

—TV news report

I.

In spring the dead drift back to us.
Rising up from the blackened snow
by the road, or heaving themselves
onto slick riverbanks, they call out
what names they have managed to keep.

Even this Jesus, crucified,
went straight (so says the creed) to hell
and back. Just a quick weekend tour,
he returned none the worse, no blood
in the wounds he kept for morbid
proof of his undying death.

But for these, the second coming
came too soon. All through the service
I see their sodden bodies turned,
their pockets searched, the call put in.

Did they, as he, say they would be
right back? And did they pray at last
for their deliverance from that—
bullet or blizzard, rage or despair—
which took them without recompense?

II.

Where, O Death, is now thy sting?
I cannot say, for that is not
my revelation. Still, I know
somewhere the squad car pulls into
the drive, or the telephone rings
and rings until it's satisfied.

As for me, I'm going to have
some turkey later, and some wine.
The Lord is risen! Pass the pie.
Those two lost souls on the TV
for whom I seem to mourn on this,
the morn for mourning's end, will be
in time to me no more than snow
that keeps their lost, curled shapes alive
awhile, then melts away. No loss
but to my memory, to some
brief notion of my own innate
capacity for sympathy.

Still, I hope that somewhere someone
keeps a grief no words allay.
The dead should ruin someone's day.

III.

Which is, when all's been said and the stone's
been rolled aside the open grave,
my own failing come Easter time—
that even in the flickering dark
that haunts the blood at Tenebrae,

I see the glint of angel fire,
of that long-promised getting up,
and lose the sharp spear-point of grief
that for a moment pierced my side
but dies almost as quickly then
when Sunday begins creeping in.

Jesus, it isn't hard enough
for us to know that you arose.
You're God; the supernatural
is your first nature, after all.
But dying—that took no magic dust.
The criminals were good at that
as you, though not by choice, of course.
We get the God part of the tale.
It's Jesus the man that makes us squirm,
not least because in him we see
ourselves up on that bloody tree.

IV.

Which version of this should I believe?
In *The Dream of the Rood*, you climb
so eagerly onto your cross,
the Germanic hero's sacrifice.
Today we'd call that suicide
by cop. I know, more blasphemy.

So here's my compromise: don't rise.
This one time don't get up. Instead,
stay dead and make us contemplate
with new resolve that hammer blow,
and then the listless dark that comes
to claim the place we hollowed out.

Let us feel the knot of panic
tighten in our chests as the hours
tick away and still the burial stone
lies heavy at your door, no glow
of angels, no gardeners lurking
in the underbrush. Let us all
pour ashes on our heads and tear
the fancy clothes clean off our backs.

Then, as the hours and days slip past,

let us begin at last to give
up hope, suspect it's all our fault,
that because of this or of that—there is
of course so much from which to choose—
you left, and you're not coming back.
Unlike the ones they found, you're lost
for good, your body left to rot
within the soon-forgotten tomb.
And where your spirit is, God knows.

V.

Reader, which is worse: to admit
that your beloved's death has taken
your life, too, and made it feel
unlivable? Or that, too soon,
life will go on as it once did,
that milk will curdle in the jar
and you, repulsed, will pour it out,
drive to the store and buy some more?

Or this small scene: a week from now,
a father hauls curbside the last
rotten stalks of funeral flowers,
then picks the Sunday paper up,
dark-spotted by the rain, and checks
to see who won the Red Sox game.

VI.

"The God who is with us is the God
who forsakes us." *Eloi, Eloi*
Lama Sabachthani. Jesus,
who loved the fallen world so much
you did not want to leave—who loved
our shit and our souls together,
our foul stink and our frankincense—

Jesus, betray us without a kiss.
Make us hate you for it. Bereft,
let us fall back to earth and curse
and gutter at you, who made us
first to turn against it. Only then
will our spoiled, human blood become
a kind of sacramental wine,
the new made mud incarnadine.

VII.

This is the new Eden after all.
The rioting thorns in flower. Our sin
is not our failure to forsake
the world, but that we do not love
the world enough. Dear Jesus, please,
don't rise until we do. And when,
among the host who fall each day,
two more declare their names, let us
all weep for them instead of you,
who taught us how, when weeping you
asked God to spare your life, to take
from you both cup and crown, in that
dark garden just outside of town.

Three

Liturgy

You came to me slowly
as light through a jar

You came as ice comes
to the surface of a lake

For forty days and forty nights
we talked with our mouths full

For an age we were lost
in the world of our eyes

At the fork in the road
we sat down to wait

At the hour of confession
we fell down into sleep

In the trees we found nothing
but the darkness of trees

In the hill-cleft the birth
we could not quite remember

We abandoned our hearts
for the cold fact of each other

We abandoned our hearts

When we crossed into shadow—
a field of lit matches

When we crossed into silence—
the uneasy silence of birds

Across Some
Smoke-Filled Room

Tell me about breath, its curl and cry,
its brief charged argument with air.
Asleep or waking, how it breaks
into lines the liturgy of hours. Say how,
in our wide surprise, we take a world
into our mouths, its shape and taste,
as if apprenticing for that
long caesura—collapsing like a lung—
between our bodies and desire.

Who was it (some philosopher
of dark apartments) who found inside
the cave of his mouth, in the damp
blue-black of it, the sad Promethean urge
to hold an afterthought of fire on his tongue?

Today, when the young priest came
to me and placed *the body*
on my tongue, I tasted the smoke
he smoked an hour ago.

It's late. This is how I talk
to myself. We haven't even met.
And the distance, all that air
between us, darkens itself
with the odd, barely believable shapes
we tether to a name.

Or I am waking up just now,

next to you, as I have for the last ten years,
and you are snoring a little
repulsively, and I can touch you—
just your hair fanning my pillow—
and I don't need you
to show me anything but that.

Kansas

So we drove all the way across Kansas
in the rearview mirror of a storm.
The radio towers hummed above us

no particular tune for a villainess
or a man without backbone or charm.
But we drove all the way across Kansas

for something—perhaps it was for this:
to prove we could only do so much harm.
Like the radio towers looming above us,

we flashed a bright warning, red and careless,
then stoic, inscrutable as the term
that we drove all the way across Kansas

to find, whether it be *love* or *weakness*.
We just wanted something obvious and firm
as the radio towers that rose above us.

But country radio is all about loss.
Kansas is about the death of the farm.
So we drove all that way, across Kansas

and back, through the heat and wind and dust,
to discover nothing left to learn.
Nothing in all that way across Kansas,
or in the radio towers above us.

Plasma

There were days when the body's hunger grew
to a shape the body could not dignify,
days when the weather, blistering, could be
reduced to the level of exchange: degrees
at odds against the window's double pane.

That was the summer, summer's end, I sold
my plasma twice a week. There, in a steel
warehouse on Douglas, all the brutal youth
of Wichita, starved and half hung-over,
unwed and unshorn, lay down in neat rows,
offered up our clean, clean blood to the world.

This was before I believed the world could be
reduced to the size of this poem, before
I knew the whole sun could ride on the back
of a pale brown bird, flitting from branch to branch.

For months, I'd witnessed my unshuttering,
my whole life becoming permeable.
So many friends passed through me, I want to name
them now, against the bare face of my own
neglect: Richard and Dennis and Tom and Ray,
Julie and Jim and Brett and all the other
Elephants, killing themselves night after night
at Kirby's Beer Store on Seventeenth Street.

And you, Therese: all winter into spring
we exhausted each other, night by night,
hoping the fever in the blood we shared
would burn away, in time, whatever ill
made us need to believe in each other.

On the gurney, I watched my blood go out,
deep red in the plastic tubing, twisting down
to where it entered the machine that whirred
and spun beside. How long this took I can't
recall. I only know after a time
I felt the pressure there reverse, something
coming back again, peregrine and strange.

Was this my blood returning, absent what
my blood could do without? I still can't say.
I only know that substance came, climbed through
and entered me. And if it was my blood
it was a colder, clearer kind than I
had ever felt or seen.
                          Though as for that,
when I emerged outside, the heat still struck
me like an open hand, and I recoiled,
returned to my dank, orange shag apartment,
slept through another dimlit afternoon,
and when a few days later I returned,
my blood ran out as ever, slow and red.
Those days I felt it was enough to lie
down for a spell, let all go slack, something
in me going out, something coming back.

Tiny Prayer for the
Redeye Flight Descending

We wake to false bell
roused singly, a tensile
and creased by pillow,
undoing we manage row
like frowsy, time-lapsed
numb faces, unfolding
into the morning
of sunrise mist, pretty
Below, the land divides
my eye believes, gives
as each brief symmetry
a flock of snow geese
below, a rolling,
inside its circle,
of white above
In their downward spiral
at a place that will
a last whirl to
let it drop, shatter,
we pass over, still
our second skin,
This is the world
Dear Jesus,

and flickering, false birth
straining, skin lined
shoulder, care, a fine
by row, fumbling forth
flowers pushing earth,
lagged and lean
of our arrival, red skein
for what it's worth.
and clusters, patterns
up, believes again,
collapses, scatters:
descending to the grain
roiling globe, alive
great tear, bright rain
the gold, spent stubble.
their only hope is to arrive
feed them as they give
the world's bright double,
a quick white scrawl
waking alive inside
our capsule, guide.
into which we must fall.
let us fall.

The Fall

It starts, like all of us, with an open mouth:
the altar boy's surprise, rush of incense,
the light chest rising. What to call the doused
fire of his lips, the quick innocence
released by his lily throat, and what calling
at the heart of his startled gasp, what song
in the clatter and slap of the great book falling?
The end, he thinks, but as that Holy Word
falls past, he catches Adam, one smooth palm
hovering there like a small, untutored bird
above her skin, before the scent of sin,
before his own body began to rise,
when all were naked, merely waders in
the unconsummated waters of paradise.

Louisiana

after Wilfred Owen

So Noah rose, with an axe went out, and felled
the forest all around, and planed the wood
and joined it also, according to the rude
assignment God had dreamed into his head.
And when that work was done, though he'd not seen
a cloud for weeks, and all was stars and sun,
he honored God, and laying a hand upon
her hull, christened the ark *Evangeline*.
Weeks passed. God's creatures all were gathered in,
and then, at last, the rain did fall, the tide
rose up, and when it reached them, Noah cried
for God to spare them from the flood's cruel end.
But God demurred, the ark was overcome,
and all the souls inside her, one by one.

Burial Amulet
with Twin Figures

In half-light of the ancient wing, we bless
her clayed figure, this formal, regal grief
the ground gave up, unbrushed in hushed relief.
The heathen moon *(4th century, impress)*
preserves the amber of slow time. We guess
what brought her down to this, what epoch strife
twin singers *(inlaid)* dirge. Their thin arms lift
the moon, suspend its arc above her chest,
solid and stark as the night-black sea. And yet,
no moon abides, no tides, no undertow.
Alone in dim lit rooms, hard amulet,
your voiceless lovers pine and trill, still know
the gesture is the thing, that art is long,
and know, at last, the dead require a song.

Twenty Answers

after "Twenty Questions" by Maura Stanton

Because I could. No not that end, the other.
The red one holding her little red shoes.
Because I'm your father and she's your mother.
Portulaca. Or possibly Moss Rose.
You can't go outside without a warm sweater.
Beside the dead squirrel. Thicker the better.
Excuse me, I thought I was holding your hand.
To me it felt warm, like a chicken's breast
beneath the pin feathers. Because it was banned.
A black bag and a piece of her yellow dress.
Because the end may come sooner than you think.
Because you're wrong. Because I need a drink.
Their babies nurse. Yes, they said it was cancer.
I've forgotten the question. I'd rather not answer.

V

A tiger's tooth; brief tickle on the lip
   before the waspy hum comes from a thrum
     in the throat's dark vespiary; cleft in the rock
where the dove lays her eggs; a little ship
   nosing its bow across white waves that comb
     the bay; between breasts, between legs, both cock
and cleavage; Nixon taking off for home;
   augur; icepick; compass; finger and thumb;
     it's how we made our first birds fly—a flock
of wings; it's how we tell the vulture from
the hawk.

Essay

In "The Boy of Winander" Wordsworth paints
the youth lakeside. He's calling out to owls
at dusk, his small hands cupped around his mouth,
and when at last they don't call back, the void
they leave resides not in the air that fails
to tremble with their song but in his own
deep double self, whose heart receives instead,
though he himself is unaware, "the voice
Of mountain torrents; or the visible scene . . .
With all its solemn imagery." All these
he carries "far into his heart," as if
the distance there conceived is not
outward at all, instead begins at the ear
or eye, the tongue or skin, whichever sense,
absent mind, gathers the impression in.

Does it matter that, in an early draft,
at the moment the owl fails to call,
Wordsworth becomes himself the boy: "my call,"
"my skill," "I hung," he says, "[l]istening" for
what never came. Or that, in later drafts,
when Wordsworth slays the boy—"was taken
from his Mates"—the third person is retained
throughout? Or how, in its final version—
a poor sequel he should have left undone—
Wordsworth returns again, as from the dead,
and stews upon the grave, which "hangs" halfway
between the valley and that uncertain sky
the boy once took into his heart as if
he were himself the steady, mirror lake?

It's but one more migration, self to other
self, "other I" our lyric turn requires.
What was it, after all, the boy desired?
Just this: to hear his coarse cry echo back
in a voice more alien and more true. It's all
any poet wants to do, our ageless task
and one more proof that Wordsworth *was* the boy
he killed, his death a mirror death of form
without matter, hard stars in the black of the lake.

Calling

Who are you? Me too.
Who are you? Me too.

In the winter half light, each breath
silvers, falls, as our feet fall—
we're barely married half a year—
across the bone-hard drifts
of our back acre. We're moving
toward the dark the border woods reserve
against the twin-bright pall
of snow and moon.
At the edge, just where the ragged
underbrush creeps out to claim
another crust of clearing, we stop.
I call. Everything listens.

Through the tangle of shadows,
a little east and far off, an echo,
then another, nearer still.
We dare not move, though I feel
your hand in the crook of my arm
squeeze a little tighter,
and I recall our first time
owling, how you joked
that I was "wooing" you,
and later, when the wood I'd stood up
wouldn't burn, you smiled and warmed
your hands above it anyway.

The shadows shiver a little, deep,
and then the louder, clearer song again,

strangely human, as if the owl sympathized
with our rough, inadequate transcription,
our trick against forgetting.

Who are you?

I feel your hand, strangely warm,
on my arm. I open my eyes.
You are there, half-asleep beside me
in the bed where we have slept
together almost ten full years.
The red line on the monitor leaps.

Me too.

It's Silas, not yet two, calling out
from his crib the words he's learned
from *Birding by Ear.* This is his favorite,
the Great Horned Owl, a kind of solo
call and response. Hearing this way,
in the blue-black fog of six o'clock,
awakened from my careless dream,
I'm almost overcome by fear
and love. In his tiny, sing-song liturgy,
I hear his certain loneliness, his waking
to a future full of empty, dimlit rooms.
But also this: his perfect faith
that somebody at last will come

and lift him into morning.

I rise before he calls again,
and when he sees my shadow fall
across the crack beneath his door
he chirps, in his new voice, my name,
the name my place in life has earned,
and I, like some great bird a-wing,
swoop down on him, whispering
his own name in return.

Walking Home on a
Friday, Early November

I am somewhere in the middle
of that brief, twelve-minute caesura
between the cluttered cave
of my office and the kitchen steaming

with love and children, whose voices will,
as they do each day, call back and forth
in a passion play starring Wonder
and Despair. And I am holding a book

out in front of me, following its poems
around the long bend of the boulevard
like a lame greyhound chasing
its Tantalus hare. Beyond

the white sky of the pages,
where anything might happen,
something dark and faster
whooshes, its invisible wake

pushing me off the white line
to which some other part of me
pays mind, and I look—my book
still ahead of me—and see how

Nature (c. 1803) is having a little fun
today, having matched exactly
the golden glow of a yellow maple
with the luminous throb of her horizon,

a brief cadence in the autumn fugue
she's been noodling these weeks,

all beauty and pity, etc. And because
I have been reading poems, have entered

that state of slow time, when each
honey syllable spreads itself
with a sweet, even gesture
on the grateful palate—

because I am thinking this way,
I can show you now, how the tree
(to my right) and the sky (far ahead)
bookend the poems' slender twin towers,

rising from wisdom into each beginning,
in their own atmosphere, in a different season.
All the color in the world—
this world—cannot collect them,

cannot enter the silence
of their blank sky, just as I never can,
never quite, will always remain
this arm's length away.

But now the light has changed, the tree
is back there losing and losing,
and when I reach out my hand
to open the green door—

already I hear them—as my one hand turns
the garish faux-gold of the knob—
laughter, laughter—my other hand
closes the book.

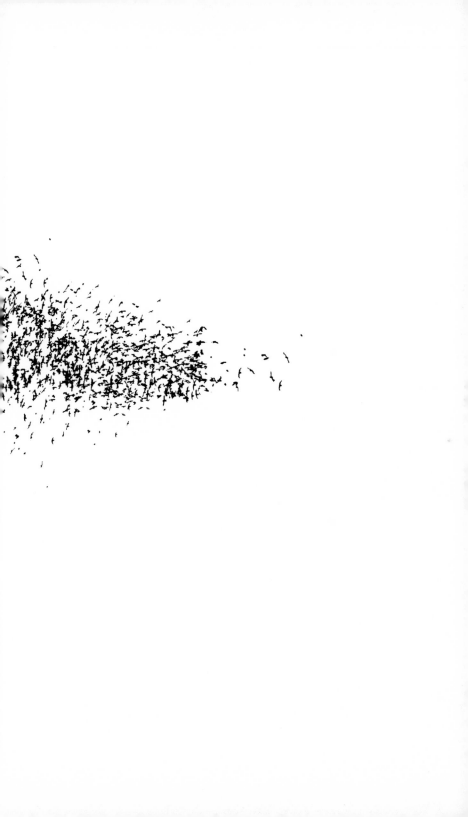